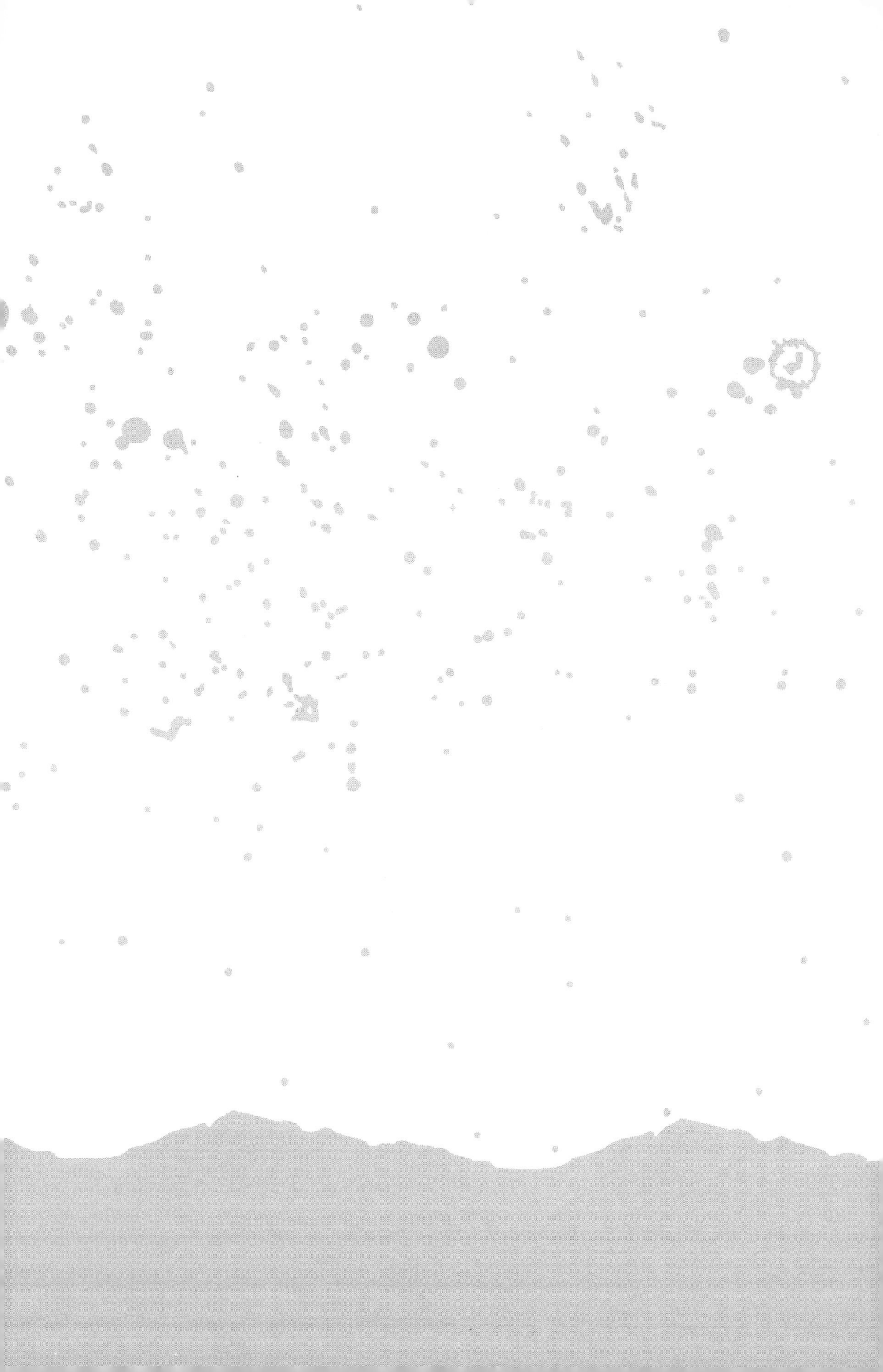

A human fart can be louder than a trombone. I discovered that at my daughter's school concert.

I made my Facebook name 'Benefits', so when you add me
now it says "you are friends with benefits"

If you know how many cupcakes I'm holding behind my back
I'll give you both of them.

I wonder how police on bike arrest people. "Alright, get in the basket"

At the end of the day life should ask us "Are you sure you want to save the changes?"

Dear phone, if you didn't light up so many times to tell me you had a low battery, you wouldn't have died so quickly.

Why didn't I use my turn signals? It's nobody's business where I'm going.

Cats have 32 muscles in each ear, to help them ignore you.

Light travels faster than sound. This is why some people appear bright until you hear them speak.

I just cleaned the house top to bottom, so now I'm gonna need everybody to stop living here.

"
I thought about
losing weight once,
but I don't like losing
"

Never go to bed angry, stay awake and plot your revenge.

It is Friday... any plan of being a productive member of society is officially thrown out the window.

Co-workers are like Christmas lights. They hang together, half of them do not work, and the other half is not so bright.

Always borrow money from a pessimist. He won't expect it back.

To be sure of hitting the target, shoot first, and, whatever you hit, call it the target.

Better to remain silent and be thought a fool than to speak out and remove all doubt.

Microsoft bought Skype for 8.5 billion! what a bunch of idiots! I downloaded it for free!

Sometimes, I spend the whole meeting wondering how they got the big meeting table through the door.

They say that love is more important than money, but have you ever tried to pay your bills with a hug?

My boss told me to start every presentation with a joke. The first slide was my paycheck.

"

Paper cut:
A tree's final
moment of revenge

"

To steal ideas from one person is plagiarism. To steal from many is research.

I don't go crazy. I am crazy. I just go normal from time to time.

Money can't buy happiness. It can, however rent it...

Every Friday, I feel like I deserve a new addition to my closet for all my hard work during the week.

Money can't buy love, but it improves your bargaining position.

Here's to another Friday of outward smiles and inward screams.

We will continue to have more meetings until we figure out why no work is getting done.

Whatever you do today, Do it with the confidence of a
4-year old wearing a Batman cape.

My bed is a magical place when I suddenly remember
everything I forgot to do.

Beat the 5 o'clock rush, leave work by noon.

"

If you don't succeed
at first, hide all
evidence that you tried

"

Wine is constant proof that God loves us and loves to see us happy.

I finally realized that people are prisoners of their phones...that's why its called a 'cell' phone.

The trouble with the rat race is that even if you win, you're still a rat.

By all means let's be open-minded, but not so open-minded that our brains drop out.

Is Google a boy or a girl? Obviously a girl because it won't let you finish your sentence without suggesting other ideas.

Evening news is where they begin with 'Good evening', and then proceed to tell you why it isn't.

I just found human hairs in my McDonald's burger. When did they start using natural ingredients?

After MONDAY and TUESDAY even, the calendar says: WTF.

Sometimes the majority only means that all the fools are on the same side.

I thought I wanted a career, turns out all I wanted is a pay check.

"————————

If Monday had a face...I will punch it

————————"

Our phones fall, we panic. Our friends fall, we laugh.

You know that moment when you get up in the morning, you're full of energy and you can't wait to get to work? Me neither!

If everyone knew what I was thinking, I would get punched in the face a lot.

Sometimes I just want someone to hug me and say "I know it's hard, but you'll be okay. Here's a coffee and a million dollars".

I followed a diet, but it didn't follow me back, so I unfollowed it.

If you think patience is a virtue, try surfing the net without high speed internet.

Starting tomorrow whatever life throws at me, I'm ducking so it hits someone else.

They say the best things take time. That is why I am always late.

The future is shaped by your dreams, so stop wasting time and go to sleep!

I lost some weight once, but I found it again in the fridge.

"

Maybe taking
a dog named shark
to the beach is
a bad idea

"

If you had to choose between eating tacos everyday or being skinny for life would you choose hard or soft tacos?

To make a mistake is human, but to blame it on someone else, that's even more human.

Tell your boss what you think about him, and the truth shall set you free, from your job.

I have been putting a lot of thought into it, and I just don't think being an adult is going to work for me.

People say I act like I don't care. It's not an act.

Don't know where your kids are in the house? Turn off the internet and they will show up quickly.

I'm a multi – tasking procrastinator. I can put off multiple things at once.

Pleasing everyone, that's impossible. Making everyone angry, piece of cake!

I'm in desperate need of a 6-month vacation twice a year.

I made a huge to do list for today. I just can't figure out who's going to do it.

" I've made it from the bed to the couch. There's no stopping me now "

They say time is the solution to every problem. I've been waiting for five hours already and the room is still messy.

Lazy is such an ugly word. I prefer to call it selective participation.

My favourite exercise is a cross between a lunge and a crunch...I call it lunch.

_____

_____

_____

_____

_____

_____

_____

_____

_____

_____

_____

_____

_____

_____

_____

_____

_____

_____

_____

If life is not smiling at you, give it a good tickling.

Your mind needs exercise just as much as your body does,
that's why I think of jogging every day.

If you love a friend, let them go. If they come back with coffee, it was meant to be.

I would go out of my mind, but I can't find the exit.

When people tell me "you're going to regret that in the morning," I sleep in until noon because I'm a problem solver.

I'm on a seafood diet, I see food and I eat it.

I'm not running away from hard work, I'm too lazy to run.

"——————————

I don't have bad handwriting, I'm just using my own font

——————————"

The only relationship I have is with my Wi-Fi. We have a connection.

Interviewer: so tell me about yourself. Me: I'd rather not...I kinda want this job.

Alcohol kills brain cells slowly, but that never bothered me because I'm not in a hurry.

People say "go big or go home" like going home is a bad thing. Heck yeah! I want to go home, and I'll have a nap when I get there.

If I had 10 cookies and you took half, do you know what you would have? That's right, a black eye and a broken hand.

For you, I would swim across the ocean. Lol, just kidding, there are sharks in there.

Stupidity is far more fascinating than intelligence, after all intelligence has it's limits.

I tried looking at the bright side of life, but it hurts my eyes.

Dear life, when I said, "can this day get any worse" It was a rhetorical question, not a challenge.

Research shows that laughing for two minutes is just as healthy as a 20minutes jog. So now I'm sitting in the park laughing at all the joggers.

"

—————————

Yes of course I am
athletic...I surf the
internet every day

—————————

"

I would have never imagined going into a bank wearing a mask and asking the teller for money.

I wonder, will lazy people go to heaven...or do they send someone to pick us up.

The difference between pizza and your opinion is that I
actually asked for pizza.

Silence is golden. Unless you have kids, then silence is just plain suspicious.

Some people aren't just missing a screw, the whole toolbox is gone.

If you don't like me, remember it's mind over matter. I don't mind and you don't matter.

Diet Rule#1: If nobody sees you eating it, it doesn't contain any calories.

I get most of my exercise these days from shaking my head in disbelief.

There's life without Facebook and internet? Really? Send me the link.

If you have an opinion about my life, please raise your hand.
Now put it over your mouth.

"

My wallet is like
an onion, opening
it makes me cry

"

A balanced diet means a cupcake in each hand.

Last night the internet stopped working so I spent a few hours with my family. They seem like good people.

I stopped understanding math when the alphabet decided to get involved.

Whoever said "out of sight, out of mind" never had a spider disappear in their bedroom.

Dear auto flushing toilet...I appreciate the enthusiasm, but I wasn't done yet.

I want someone who will look at me the same way I look at chocolate cake.

Your secrets are safe with me...I wasn't even listening.

Do I run? Yes...out of time, patience, and money.

People said follow your dreams, so I went back to bed.

Some people have "aha" moments, I just have "oh seriously?" moments.

"

I really want to
be nice, but annoying
people just won't let me

"

You come from dust and you'll return to dust, so that's why I never dust. It could be someone I know.

Sometimes the first step to forgiveness is realizing that the other person is completely stupid.

Be careful when you follow the masses. Sometimes the M is silent

Maybe if we tell people the brain is an app, they'll start using it.

You have Facebook? Yup. You have WhatsApp? Yup. You have love? Forgot to install it.

If I won the award for laziness, I would send someone to pick it up for me.

Me and my bed are perfect for each other, but my alarm clock keeps trying to break us up.

I wish my wallet came with free refills.

They say water is the source of life, which is true because you can't make coffee without water.

If we shouldn't eat at night, why is there a light in the fridge?

"
It may look like
I'm doing nothing
but in my head
I'm quite busy
"

I just tried my summer wardrobe. The only thing I managed to get into was a state of panic.

_____

_____

_____

_____

_____

_____

_____

_____

_____

_____

_____

_____

_____

_____

_____

_____

_____

_____

Who says nothing is impossible? I 've been doing nothing for years.

I changed my password everywhere to 'incorrect', that way when I forget it, it always reminds me, "your password is incorrect".

Got up this morning and ran around the block five times.
Then I got tired, so I put the block back in the toy box.

Don't drink to forget me, you'll end up seeing me double.

I'm multi-tasking: I can listen, ignore and forget at the same time.

Officer: I had a feeling I'd catch someone speeding here.
Driver: I know, that's why I came as fast as I could.

Sometimes I wish I was an octopus, so I could slap eight people at once.

If you are hotter than me, then that means I'm cooler than you.

Did you just fall? No, I was checking if gravity still works.

"

I'm not suffering
from insanity,
I'm enjoying every
minute of it

"

You never realize what you have until it's gone. Toilet paper is a good example.

I had an extremely busy day, converting oxygen into cardon dioxide.

Never go to bed angry, stay awake and plot your revenge.

Dear math, please grow up and solve your own problem I'm tired of solving them for you.

I would like to apologize to anyone whom I haven't offended yet. Please be patient, I will get to you shortly.

Sometimes the majority only means that all the fools are on the same side.

A good lawyer knows the law, a clever one takes the judge to lunch.

A cop pulled me over and told me "papers", so I said "scissors, I win!" and drove off.

Don't worry if plan A fails, there are 25 more letters in the alphabet.

Just because it's called makeup, it doesn't mean it should make up 100% of your face.

> "If you can't get people to listen, tell them it's confidential!"

If someone doesn't see you in their future, maybe it's time
to put them in your past...

When my boss asked me who is the stupid one, me or him? I told him.. Everyone knows he does not hire stupid people...

One way to stop people from jumping down your throat is to keep your mouth shut...

_____

_____

_____

_____

_____

_____

_____

_____

_____

_____

_____

_____

_____

_____

_____

_____

_____

_____

_____

_____

They say that love is more important than money, but have you ever tried to pay your bills with a hug?

If you can't get people to listen, tell them it's confidential!

Some people come into our lives & leave footprints on our hearts. Others come into our lives & make us wanna leave footprints on their face...

Never take life seriously. Nobody gets out alive anyway...

The best vitamin to be a happy person is B1...

Some people deserve a high five. In the face. With a chair...

I'm so clever that sometimes I don't understand a single
word of what I'm saying...

66

I don't fall,
I'm just spending
some quality time
with the floor

99

You love flowers, but you cut them. You love animals, but you eat them. You tell me you love me, so now I'm scared.

I think my soulmate might be carbs.

Them: money does not bring happiness. Me: pass the money over here, I like to be sad.

Never feel bad when people roll their eyes while you talk to them. They are just looking for their brain.

Always run away from temptations...but slowly, so they can catch up to you.

Life is a pretty cheesy game, but at least it has good graphics.

I want to change my name on Facebook to "Nobody", so when I see someone posting something stupid I can like their post and it will say "Nobody like this".

I don't mean to brag, but I just put together a puzzle in 1 day and the box said 2- 4 years.

My goal this weekend is to move...just enough so people don't think am dead.

Whenever I have a headache I take 2 aspirin and keep away from children, just like it says on the bottle.

"

Of course I talk to myself ... sometimes I need expert advice

"

I want to sit and read, take a nap and snack. Basically, I want to be in kindergarten.

I'll call it a smart phone when I yell "where's my phone?" and it yells back "down here in the couch cushions!"

Maybe if we all sit extremely still, Monday won't be able to see us.

I don't understand why judges get paid so much, others judge me for free.

I enjoy taking long romantic walks, to the fridge.

Sometimes I pretend to be normal, but it gets boring so I go back to being myself.

I always say "morning" instead of "good morning" because if it was a good morning, I'd still be asleep.

Sure, I do marathons. On Netflix.

Does refusing to go to the gym count as resistance training?

I hate when people text "call me". I'm going to start calling people back and as soon as they answer, I'll say "text me" then hung up.

"

I keep pressing
the space bar,
but I'm still
on earth

"

I'm not afraid to die. I just don't like the thought of being gone so long!

My mind not only wanders, sometimes it leaves completely.

I'm not lazy, I'm on power saving mode.

Your eyes water when you yawn because you miss your bed and it makes you sad.

My hobbies includes eating and complaining that I've gained too much weight.

Have some patience, I'm screwing things up as fast as possible

My silence spoke a thousand words, but you never heard them.

Due to intense brain fog all of my thoughts have been grounded until further notice.

Exercise? I thought you said extra fries!

I swallowed an ice cube yesterday and I haven't pooped it yet. I'm really scared, you guys.

"
_____

Doing nothing is hard, you never know when you are done

_____
"

I'm a ninja! No, you're not. Did you see that? See what? Exactly!

What I do when I see someone pretty is, I stare, I smile
then when I get tired I put the mirror down.

Whoever said great things come in small packages hasn't seen my big screen TV.

No, no, I'm listening, it just takes me sometime to process so much stupidity all at once.

Yes officer I saw the speed limit, I just didn't see your car.

I think I may need professional help... A chef, a butler and a maid should be enough.

I want to be cuddled, but I also want to be left alone. Being crazy is hard.

My kitchen cleaner says "for a clean kitchen" so I can't use it, mine is dirty.

I child proofed my house but the kids still get in somehow.

Nine out of ten people love chocolate, and the 10th person is always lying.

"

I'm great in bed..
I can sleep for days.

"

If you think nothing is impossible, try slamming a revolving door.

After a while, I eventually fell in love and there was nobody to pick me up.

My neighbour asked if he could use my lawnmower and I told him of course he could, So long as he didn't take it out of my garden.

Dance like nobody is watching, because they are not, they are all checking their phones.

I am grateful that my thoughts don't appear as bubbles over our heads.

The problem with drinking and driving is that trees defend themselves very well.

I'm glad I don't have to hunt my own food, I don't even know where sandwiches live.

Have you ever tried to eat a clock? It's very time consuming.

You know your driving is really terrible when your GPS says "after 300 feet, stop and let me out!"

An apple a day keeps anyone away, if you throw it hard enough.

"———————

I'm slowly
becoming an adult...
please make it stop.

——————— "

I wasn't mad, but now that you asked me 7 times if I'm mad...yes, I'm mad!

My cell phone is acting up, I keep pressing the home button but when I look around, I'm still at work.

All my life I thought air was free, until I bought a bag of chips.

I did not trip and fall. I attacked the floor and I believe I am winning.

I'm staying up past midnight this New Year's Eve. Not to welcome the new year, but to make sure this one is over.

Skinny jeans are like calories. Easy to put on but impossible to take off...

For me math class is like watching a foreign movie without subtitles.

You can stop driving me crazy, I can walk from here.

I don't know how to act my age because I've never been this old before.

I may not know karate, but I know crazy and I'm not afraid to use it.

Printed in Poland
by Amazon Fulfillment
Poland Sp. z o.o., Wrocław
13 July 2022

2716f490-761b-4e53-8724-d10f43f97fb0R02